Donated to
SAINT PAUL PUBLIC LIBRARY

Make
Me a
Peanut
Butter
Sandwich

and a
glass of
milk

Ken
Robbins

SCHOLASTIC INC.
New York

PHOTO CREDITS:

Page 15: U.S. Wheat Associates, Photo by Jerry Taube
Page 16: U.S. Wheat Associates

Library of Congress Cataloging-in-Publication Data
Robbins, Ken.
Make me a peanut butter sandwich (and a glass of milk) / Ken Robbins.
   p.   cm.
Summary: Text and hand-tinted photographs show how each part of a
peanut butter sandwich and milk for lunch is made, from field, to store,
to table.
   ISBN 0-590-43550-7
   1. Peanut butter—Juvenile literature.   2. Bread—Juvenile
literature.   3. Wheat—Juvenile literature.   4. Peanuts—Juvenile
literature.   5. Milk—Juvenile literature.   [1. Peanut butter.
2. Bread.   3. Wheat.   4. Peanuts.   5. Milk]   I. Title.
TX814.5.P38R63   1992
641.6'56596—dc20   90-23532
                                                          CIP
                                                          AC

12 11 10 9 8 7 6 5 4 3 2 1   2 3 4 5 6 7/9

Printed in the U.S.A.   36

First Scholastic printing, September 1992

Designed by Marijka Kostiw

For Faith

ACKNOWLEDGEMENTS:

Food production is a big business, and many of the corporate giants of the industry were unwilling to have their operations photographed or even (in some cases) witnessed. Special thanks are due, therefore, to the generous people with nothing to hide who invited me in to see and record what they do.

In particular, I am grateful to Mr. Jack White of the Apple White Farm, the owners of the Worrell Farm, and the owner of Fox Farms—all in Capron, Virginia; Mr. Harvey Pope, owner, and Mr. Mark Hodges III, of the Handcock Peanut Company, in Courtland, Virginia; and Mr. Eddie Marks of the Virginia—Carolina Peanut Farmers Co-op, in Franklin, Virginia; in Albany, New York, Mr. Wayne Freihofer, Ed McNall, and Dick McNeill, all of the Charles Freihofer Baking Company; Craig Edling, and particularly Mr. Antonio Scippa of Bay State Milling in Clifton, New Jersey; John Henry Kanach and Jim Clark at Rainbow Valley Farm in Flemington, New Jersey; Lisa Godino; John A. Du Fosse, owner of The Now or Never Farm in Ringoes, New Jersey; Richard Classey, Vice President and General Manager of the Oaktee Dairy in East Northport, New York; Shirley Wirth, Dena Long, Bob Anderson, and the people at Walnut Acres, in Penn's Creek, Pennsylvania; and Mr. Pardini of King Kullen Supermarkets.

Other people went out of their way to be informative and helpful, and I am grateful to all of them: Among many others are: Bonnie Kurtz and Kim Cutchins at the Peanut Butter Council in Alexandria, Virginia; Mr. Ed Johnston at the New York Department of Agriculture; Zin Samuel at the New Jersey Department of Agriculture; Gordon Tjelmeland of Deere & Company in Moline, Illinois; and Sheila Buff of Ibid Editorial Services in New York City. Closer to home, Doug Kuntz and Lauren Jarrett, Lise King and Zephyr Jost were all particularly helpful.

K.R.

Everyone knows that the best after-school snack is a peanut butter sandwich and a glass of milk. But did anyone ever stop to think about where this favorite snack came from? Of course the milk came from the refrigerator, and the peanut butter and the bread from the cupboard. But where did these crucial ingredients *really* come from, before they got to the supermarket? The truth is they've actually come a long way before they wind up in a sandwich. In fact ...

Peanut butter starts out as seeds. Farmers take these seeds and plant them. Virginia and Georgia are two good places for them to grow.

What are peanut seeds? Peanuts!

Once planted, the peanut seeds grow into bushes about two feet tall. Then the bushes grow stalks that bend over and push back into the ground. New peanuts grow on the ends of these stalks. The peanuts are covered with shells and grow down in the soil. That's why peanuts are sometimes called *groundnuts*.

In the fall, the peanut plants are pulled from the ground and left to dry in long piles known as *windrows*.

When the windrows are dry, a special truck called a *combine* separates the peanuts from the rest of the plant and dumps them into a trailer.

Trucks carry the peanuts to a building called a *shellery.*

There the peanuts are removed from their shells.

Next, the shelled peanuts are roasted in special ovens. The roasting makes them taste better.

Last of all, the roasted peanuts are crushed into peanut butter by a grinding machine, and the peanut butter is put into jars.

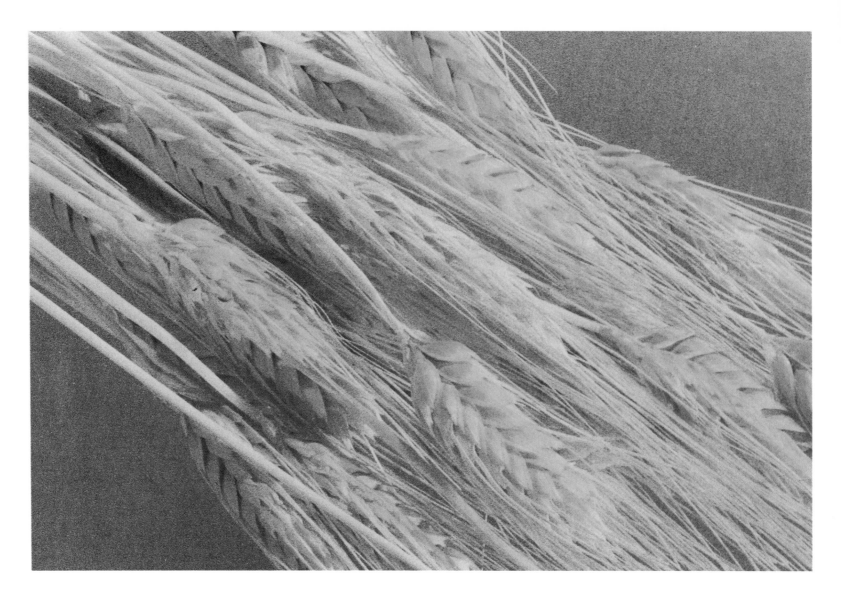

The process of making bread begins when a farmer plants some wheat. Like the peanuts, wheat grows from a seed and produces more seeds. It's the seeds, or kernels, that eventually become bread. Wheat grows well in states like Nebraska and Oklahoma.

When the wheat is grown and ready to be harvested, farmers drive combines through the fields. These machines cut down the wheat and separate the kernels from the rest of the plant.

The kernels, or grain, are stored in special tall buildings until they are needed. These buildings are called *silos* or *elevators*. They keep the grain from going bad.

When it is needed, the grain is shipped to a mill, where rows and rows of milling machines grind it into a fine white powder called *flour.*

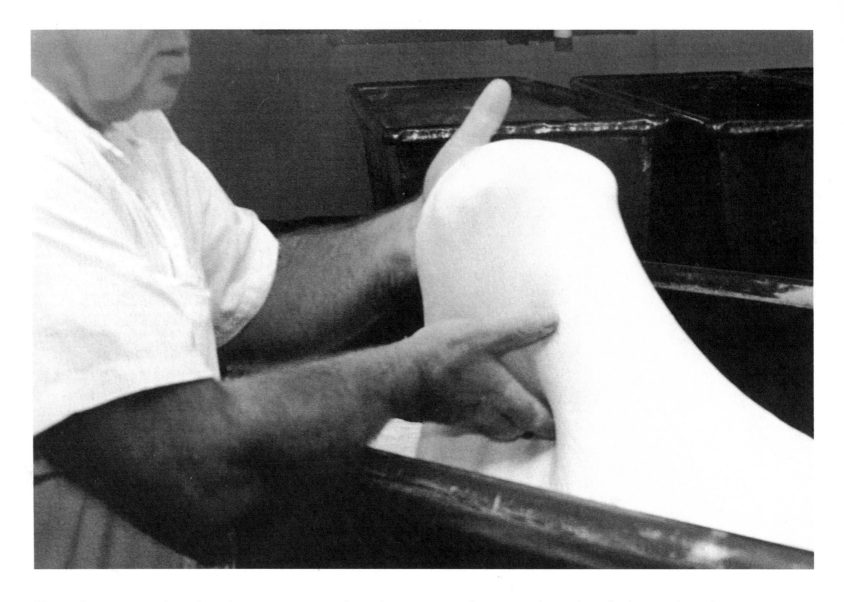

Flour becomes dough when it is mixed with water and yeast. At a big bakery, dough is made in large batches and then it is left to rest in a warm, dark place. During that time, the yeast makes the dough expand to almost twice its size.

Now that it is ready for baking, the dough is divided into small loaves and placed in baking pans. The filled pans move through the oven on conveyor belts.

The conveyor belt goes at a certain speed so the loaves come out on the other side of the oven, golden brown and done just right.

Next, the loaves go through a special slicing machine.

Then, each loaf is individually wrapped. It's finally ready for the market.

Milk, of course, comes from cows that have recently had calves.

Milk cows are raised on dairy farms. In good weather, they are able to graze on the sweet grass in the fields. In bad weather, the dairy farmer must feed them grain.

Twice a day, the cows are brought into the barn. Usually they are locked into narrow stalls, so they can't run away or kick while they are being milked.

Dairy farmers attach a special milking machine to the cows' teats. The machine squeezes the teats just the way a baby calf would.

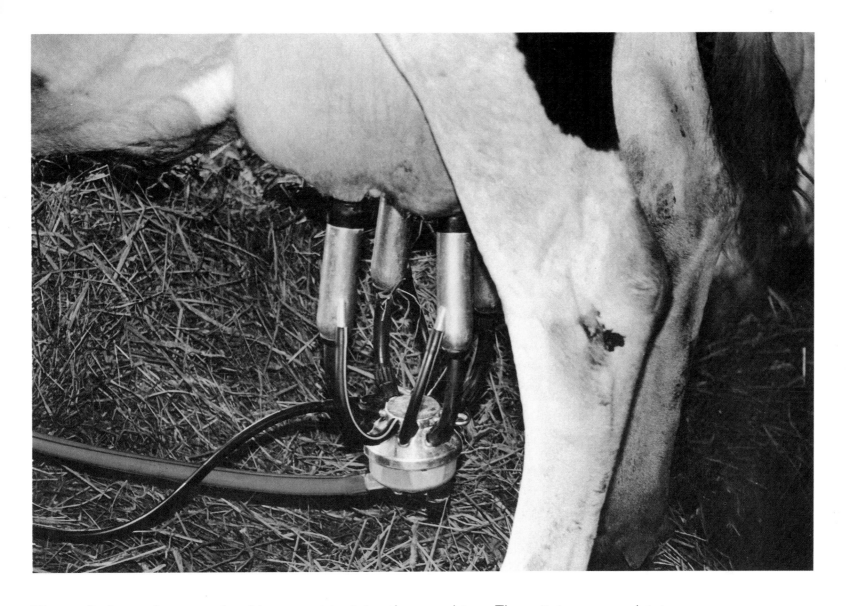

The milk from the cows' udders squirts into the machine. Then it is pumped into a refrigerated tank where it is kept cool.

A special tanker truck takes away the milk.

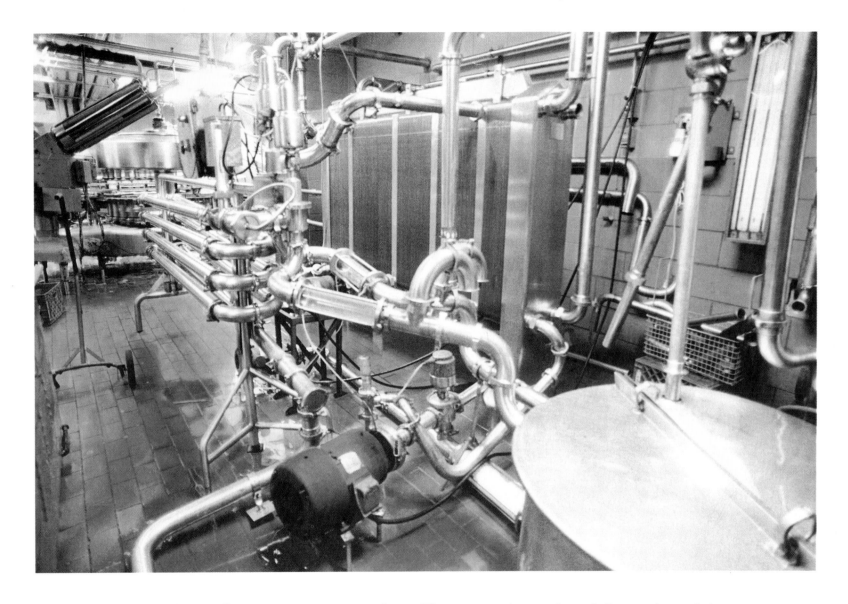

The truck brings the milk to a processing plant. There it is heated to kill any harmful germs. This is called *pasteurization*.

After it is pasteurized, the milk is ready to be put into bottles or cartons.

At last, the milk is shipped to the supermarket. That's where all three items, the peanut butter, the bread, and the milk, come together for the first time. And, of course, that's where someone from your family goes shopping.

All that work for a peanut butter sandwich and a glass of milk!